What is a community

by Edward Radlauer and Ruth Shaw Radlauer

illustrated by N. Kay Stevenson

ELK GROVE PRESS, INC. Chicago, Los Angeles

What is a community?

CHAPTER	PAGE
1. WHAT IS A COMMUNITY?	1
2. PEOPLE HELP EACH OTHER	6
3. COMMUNITIES GROW AND CHANGE	10
4. COMMUNITIES ARE NOT ALIKE	18
5. COMMUNITIES HELP EACH OTHER	20
6. COMMUNITIES NEED LAWS	24
7. PEOPLE MAKE LAWS	26
8. PEOPLE PAY TAXES	28
9. PEOPLE IN COMMUNITIES HELP EACH OTHER	32
10. COMMUNITIES BUILD SCHOOLS	38
11. PEOPLE PLAY	44
12. PEOPLE WORK	48
13. PEOPLE MOVE ABOUT	50
14. YOUR FAMILY AND THE COMMUNITY	54

What is a community?

Where do you live?

Do you live in a house like this,

or this?

Do you live in an apartment like this,

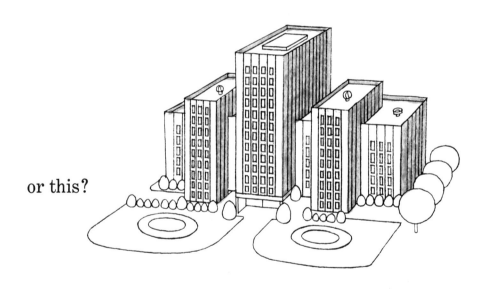

or this?

Perhaps your home is a trailer like this one.

You and your friends live in houses,

or apartments, or trailers,

on a street, or a road at the edge of town.

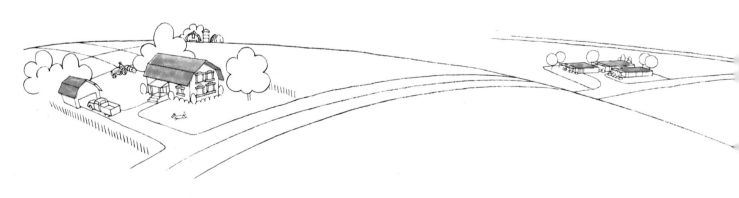

Wherever you live, you are part of a community. Can you find your street or road on a map of your community?

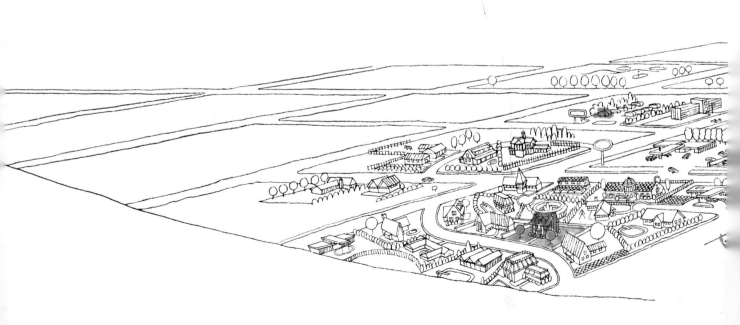

What is a community and how did communities come about? A community is the place you and your friends and their families live. A community is where people live and work together to make their lives safe and healthy, happy and comfortable.

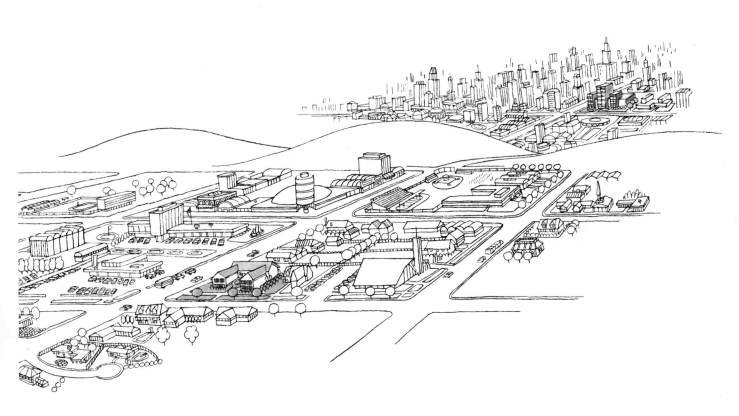

People help each other

Long ago when a man lived in a cave with his family, he hunted wild animals to eat. He used their skins for clothes. His wife gathered wild grains and fruit to feed the family. If they could not get enough food, they went hungry.

One day people discovered that by working together they could help each other and protect themselves from animals and people who were their enemies. They found that men who hunted together could catch more food. The women worked together looking for grains and other plant foods. When men discovered they could plant seeds, they began to farm. Women working together in the fields could watch their children while they worked. The older children helped, too.

As they grouped together, they formed villages or communities. One man was a better farmer, one man a better tool maker, and one a better hunter. Working together they could make their lives safer and more comfortable. Each person could share what he did best with others.

When people fought among themselves, they knew they needed rules or laws to follow. There have been communities where one man made all the rules. There have been communities where one man took what he wanted because he was stronger or smarter than everyone else. There have been places where everyone had to worship in the same way. Sometimes people leave communities like these and try to make a new home somewhere else. Many of the first communities in the United States were started by people who wanted a better way of living together.

Communities grow and change

Your community began in a country where every man could help decide what his community would be like. It began when a few families found a place with good soil and water. As more people came, a man built a store to sell things. Together the people built a church.

Their children needed a school and a teacher.

They needed someone to govern the town,

so they elected a mayor and a council. A sheriff

was needed to protect people and property.

Then they built a town hall which had offices where the council and the mayor could work. The sheriff had his office in the town hall and there was a big room where the people could meet.

A community out in the country surrounded by farms is called a *rural* community. People from the farms came into the village to buy things they could not make or grow. They sold their produce to the people in the village. They came to go to school and

church, to visit friends, and do their banking and other business. This made the village grow.

Some villages grew so large they became big cities where thousands of people lived and worked. A city is called an *urban* community.

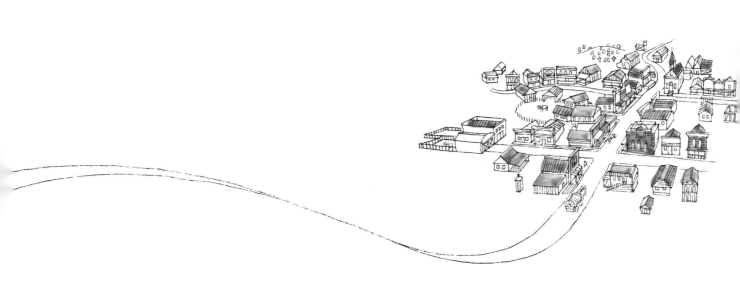

As cities grew noisier and more crowded, families moved farther from the center. As they moved out, they bought land in rural areas. Each rural community grew so large it touched the one next to it. That town may have grown, too, and reached the community on the other side.

Today there are many smaller towns around most big cities. They are near the urban community, so we call them *suburban* communities, or *suburbs*.

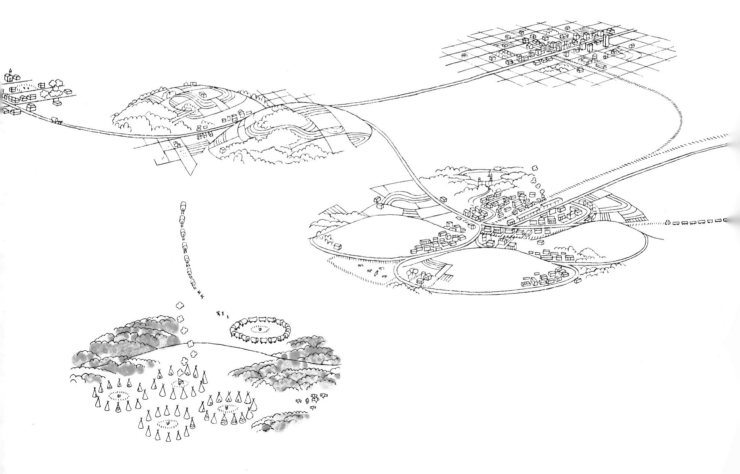

As rural communities grew into suburbs, fields and orchards were used to build houses. New streets and roads were added. More schools were needed. The libraries needed to be bigger. New churches were built. Perhaps you have watched your community grow from year to year.

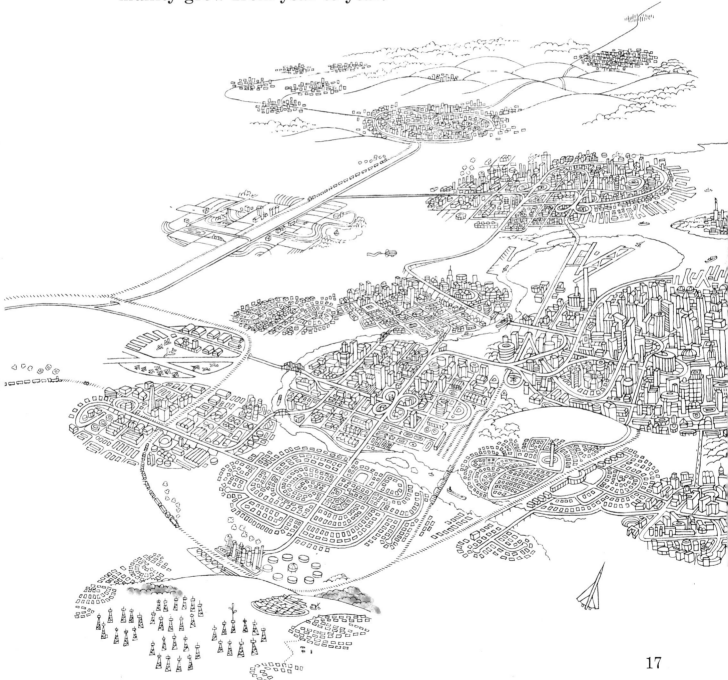

Communities are not alike

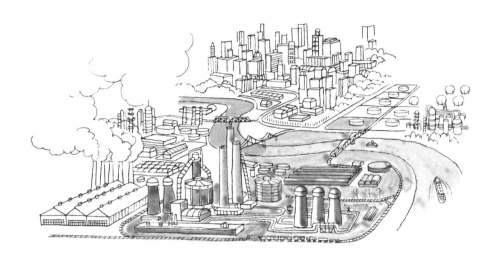

Is your community exactly like the one next to it? The next town may be very much like yours; perhaps there are more factories in the one closer to the big city. Your town may have a college with a big campus like a park and many buildings for the students. It may have less smoke than the community with factories. It may be cooler because it is near the ocean.

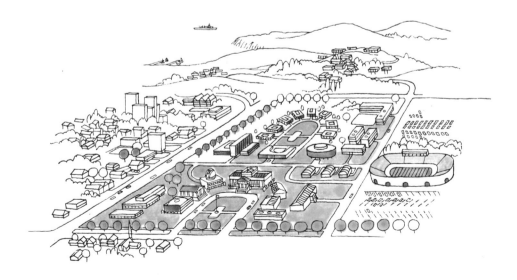

It may have houses like these, or it may have houses with big

yards and gardens.

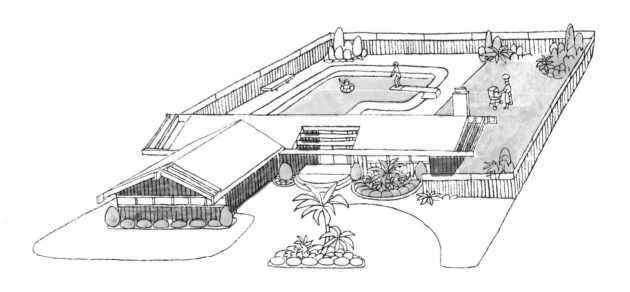

Communities help each other

At first, farmers got their water from wells or streams. They carried it to the house in buckets. Then someone invented pumps, and water was pumped through pipes into the houses. As more people came, the community needed more water. If there was a river or big wells near the town, the citizens voted to build a pumping station to bring water to the village or farms.

Many cities do not have a river or enough rain water to keep wells full, so they join together to build large pipes and trenches called aqueducts. They build pumping stations to bring water through these aqueducts from faraway rivers.

When it rains too much, the town may have floods. Then people plan ways to save the water as well as keep it from flooding their homes.

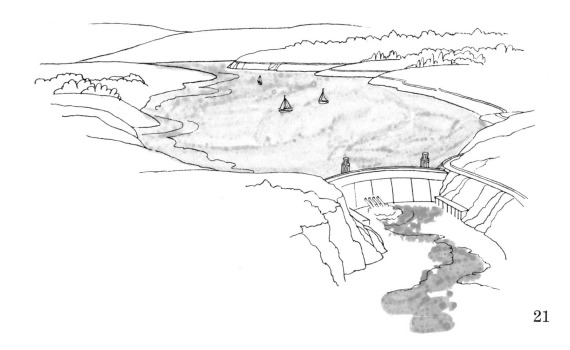

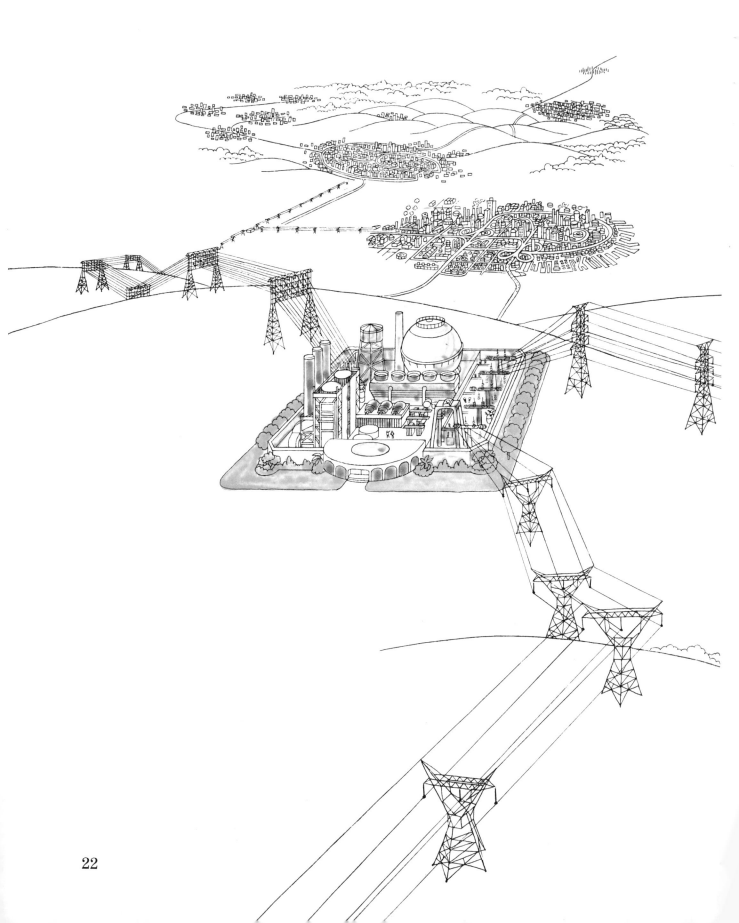

When electricity was discovered, families wanted to use it to light their homes and run machines. An electric generator costs too much for one family to own, so people put their money together and formed an electric company. The company built generators to make enough electricity to sell to everyone. A big electric company sells to more than one community.

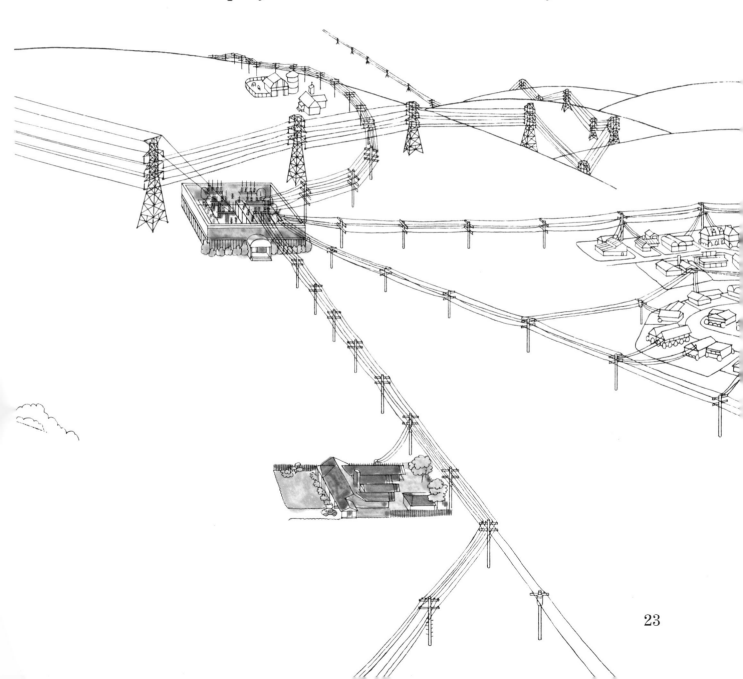

Communities need laws

Why do we need laws and rules? If you lived alone on an island you would not need laws. What would happen if there were two other people on the island with you? The three of you would need rules to help you get along with one another.

Do you need rules in your classroom? Imagine what your school would be like without them. How would it be if everyone came to school when he wanted and went home when he felt like it?

With so many automobiles on the streets should each driver make his own traffic laws?

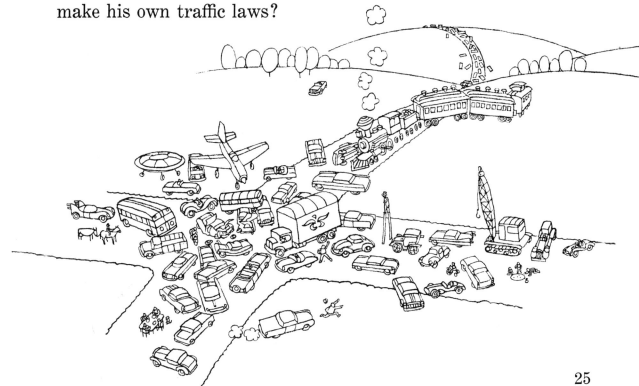

People make laws

To make your community safe, comfortable and beautiful, the citizens meet together to make laws.

Mother and Father do not always decide what the laws will be. They vote for the men and women who make the laws.

All the men and women in your community vote to choose the city council. In some cities the council chooses one of its members to be the mayor. In other cities the people elect the mayor.

The mayor is the head of the city government. He works with

the council to make the rules which we call laws or ordinances.

He works with the Fire Chief, the Chief of Police and the head

of all city departments. Some laws are made by the state, and

some by the county. Others are made by the leaders of our country.

The mayor and the city council make the ordinances for your city.

NATIONAL

STATE

COUNTY

CITY

People pay taxes

Think of all the people who work to run your community. The mayor has a family for whom he must buy food and clothing. Teachers and other school workers, policemen and firemen have families, too. How does the city pay them for all their work?

To pay for all these services, the citizens in your community pay a certain amount of money called taxes. There are three main kinds of taxes, *property* taxes, *sales* taxes, and *income* taxes.

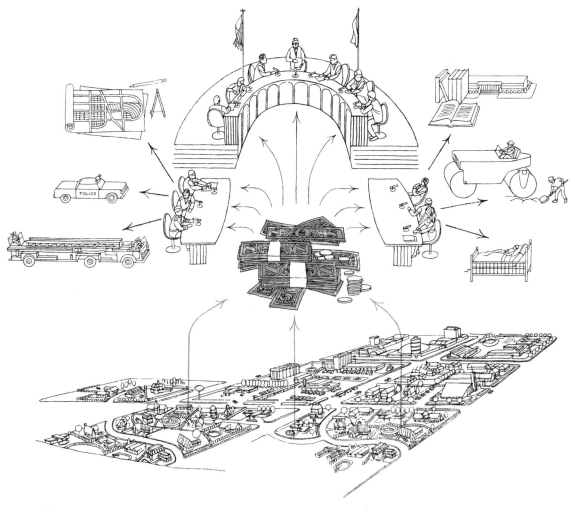

PROPERTY TAXES

A man who owns property pays a property tax. One who owns a big apartment house pays a larger tax than someone who owns a small house. You can see why a man with more valuable property pays more taxes.

Your city or county collects a property tax to pay for such things as libraries, streets, and police cars.

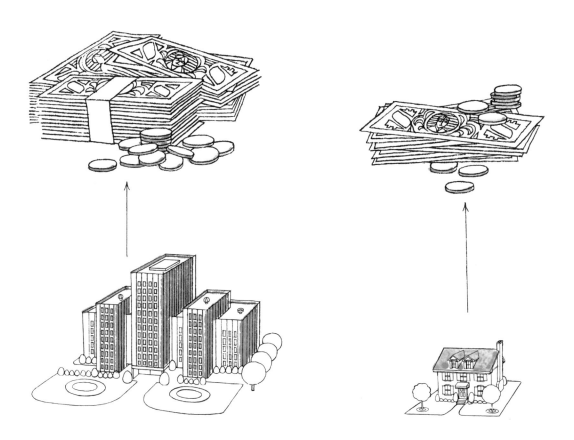

SALES TAXES

When you buy some things, you pay a sales tax. You might pay two or four cents every time you spend a dollar on clothes, toys, or candy. Some of this money is paid to your city and some to your state. The state puts all its tax money together to help pay for the cost of running the state, building roads, and helping your community pay for school buildings.

INCOME TAXES

People who work pay taxes on the money they earn. This is called income tax, and it is paid to our country's government. Some cities and states also collect income taxes.

Think about the people who must be paid to run our country. The Post Office and the people who work there are paid with tax money. What other things might be paid with income taxes?

Your mother and father vote to elect people who help decide how taxes should be used. What do you suppose they do when they think taxes are too high or that the city needs to spend money on a new community center?

Communities help each other

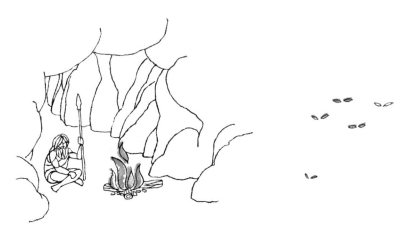

POLICEMEN HELP

How nice it is to wake up in the morning happy and safe. The cave man had to keep a fire burning at the door of his home all night to keep dangerous animals away. He had to protect his food supply from people who might come and take it.

Your family can sleep safely through the night because your community pays the police to protect your home. Imagine the work policemen do while you sleep.

When you go to school on the bus, you are sure the streets are safe. If you walk to school, you can cross the streets with a police-man or crossing guard who signals the cars and trucks to stop when you cross.

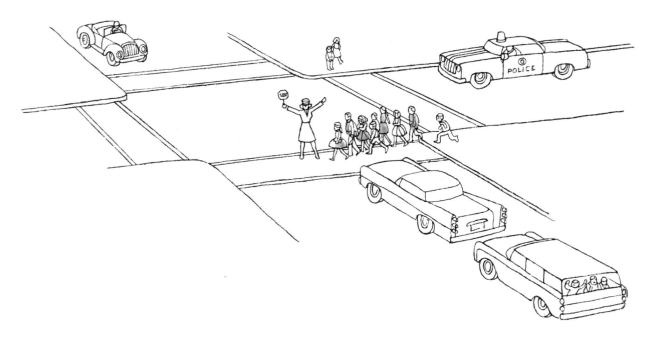

FIREMEN HELP US

Long ago there were many more fires in your town. When a fire started, someone ran to tell the leader of the fire fighters. He probably jumped out of bed and ran to the fire wagon in his night-shirt.

As the horses galloped along the streets, volunteers jumped on the wagon and rode to the fire. Other men and women ran to help. They formed a line and passed buckets of water from the wagon to the fire. They may have had more than one line and more than one wagon. Often there were not enough volunteers to put out the fire before the house or store burned to ashes.

One day the people decided their community needed a fire department, so they voted to have one as part of their city's services.

Now we have modern and fast ways to fight fires. We also have building codes. There are laws that builders must follow to make houses and other buildings safe from fire and other dangers.

Firemen inspect buildings to see there are no fire hazards. They check wiring and storage places.

HELP WITH HEALTH

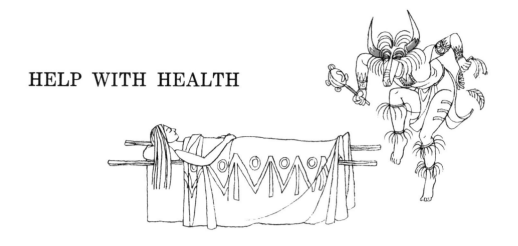

Early men did not know much about health. Some communities had witch doctors who tried to help people get well when they were sick or hurt. Men worked and learned more about the human body. Then communities had doctors to help. By the time you came to your community, doctors had learned how to prevent many diseases and accidents.

Communities now have health departments where people can have vaccinations, x-rays, and health tests to prevent many diseases. Workers from the health department check restaurants

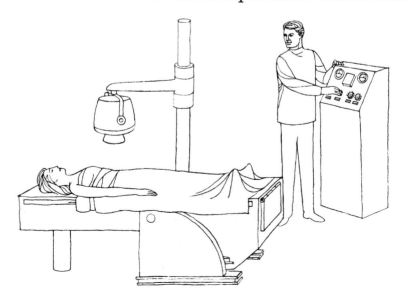

and food stores to make sure they are clean, and the people who work there must be clean and healthy. They check the city's water supply to make sure the water is pure. Some health departments check new buildings and houses to make sure they are safe.

The city council works for a healthier community when it passes laws about trash collection or smog control.

Communities build schools

After a safe night's sleep

and a good warm breakfast,

it is time to go to school.

Father goes to work to do his job

and you have a job, too.

So out the door you go

and walk to the corner

to wait for the school bus.

Like a big yellow vacuum cleaner,

it comes rumbling down the street

to sweep-up you and your friends

and take you to school.

When you get to school the principal is there. His secretary is in the office to help you.

Ladies in the cafeteria are getting food ready for lunch.

Some of the teachers are on the playground to watch you play and help you remember the safety rules.

Other teachers are writing on chalkboards and getting your classrooms ready for your learning day.

Why are all these people working? Who paid for the school building? Who pays for the teachers and principal and all the other people who run your school? Who decides what boys and girls need to learn? Who chooses the teachers and helps them decide how to help you learn to read and write, to learn about numbers, and be good citizens?

First of all, your mother and father and other adults in your community voted to elect a school board.

The people who are elected to the school board are men and women who live in your community. Your father could be a member of the school board.

The school board members meet to study and talk about the schools. They are not paid for the hours they work to plan the running of your school.

The board chooses a superintendent who directs the schools just as the mayor directs the city. The superintendent chooses the principals and teachers; and the school board votes whether to accept his choice.

SCHOOL
BOARD

SUPERINTENDENT
OF SCHOOLS

PRINCIPALS

TEACHERS

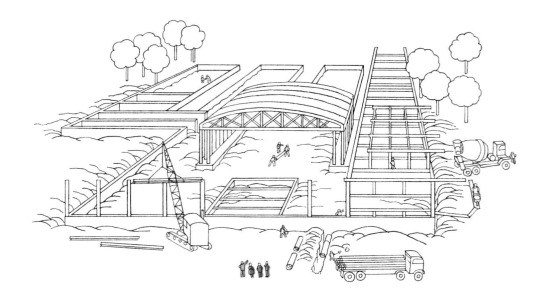

The school board members listen to the people who elected them so your community can have the kind of schools most of the people want. The board plans the building of new schools as the community grows.

If your community needs more money to build a school or pay for more teachers, the school board has a bond election so the people may decide whether or not they can pay taxes to get the extra money.

People play

Not long ago your community was probably smaller with fewer people. Boys and girls could play baseball on land that had not been used to build houses or apartments. In those days, people could walk to the edge of town, or hike to the country for a picnic.

44

As towns grew closer together, the country was covered with houses. Some communities needed places for playing, hiking, and watching games, track meets, or rodeos.

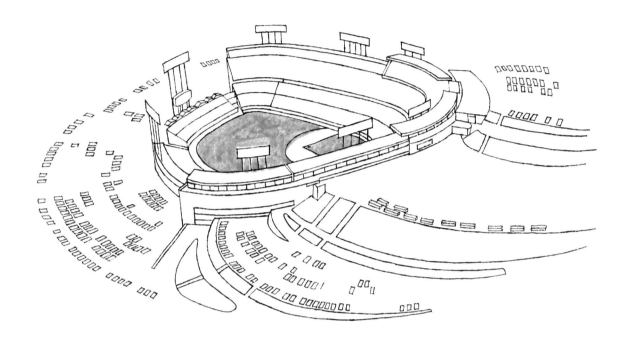

Sometimes people got together and bought land for a ball park. They charged money to watch games. This helped pay for the land and gave the owners a way to earn money.

A city often uses tax money to buy land for parks and ball fields. A state may use tax money to buy land for camping or picnic grounds.

If the state is near the ocean, the citizens may vote to use some of the taxes to build small boat harbors. Tax money pays for the people who work in these places.

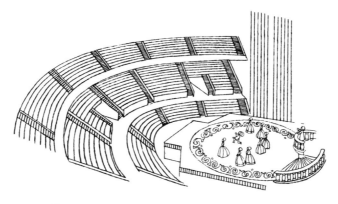

Does your town have an auditorium where you can hear concerts or see plays? Does your community have a recreation center?

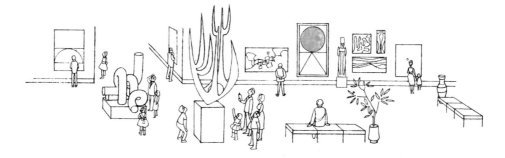

Are there museums and art galleries near you? These places are usually paid for by taxes your family and other people pay.

People work

Why do people work? As you may remember, early man worked to get food, to make clothes of skin or grass, and to build shelter. It took most of his time, and every member of the family helped.

Later people worked at one or two things. A man who was good at making tools became a specialist in tool-making. A man who did sheep herding became a shepherd. Then he traded a sheep for wheat grown by the farmer, or he might give the sheep's wool to a mason in exchange for a stone fireplace.

Now a sheep herder sells his sheep

to a packing house for money

and sells the wool to a spinning mill.

The people who own the mill pay the workers

who tend the spinning machines.

The workers use the money they earn

to pay for the things their families need.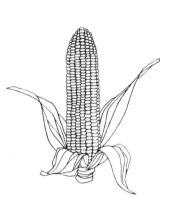

A man may have a product like corn to sell.

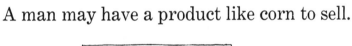

Another man might sell his work or service.

A carpenter sells his work.

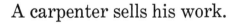

A television repair man sells his service.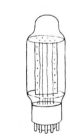

People move about

A rural community had one road. There were paths and small streets leading away from the road. What happens to roads and paths when more and more people move to the community?

The community becomes a town or small city. More people move about. More trucks bring food and clothing and carry goods from the town or other towns. Soon the streets must be made wider and smoother.

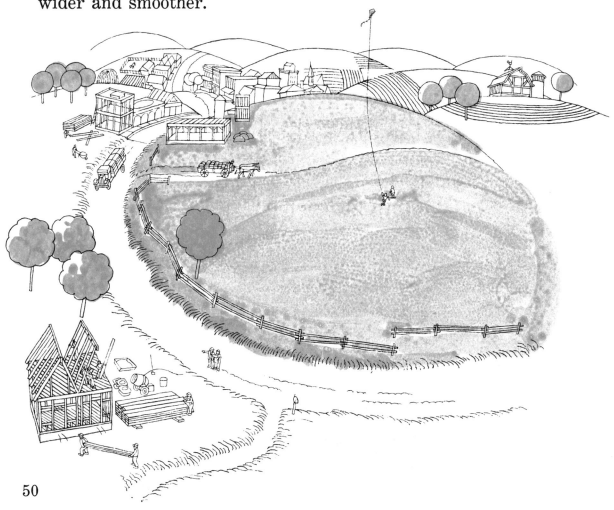

Men called traffic engineers decide where new roads are needed. They know where to build highways and wide streets.

Maybe you have watched a street being paved with asphalt or cement. Perhaps there is a highway being built near you. The land for widening the streets or building a highway must be bought from the owners. The materials to pave the street cost money, and so do the men and machines who do the work.

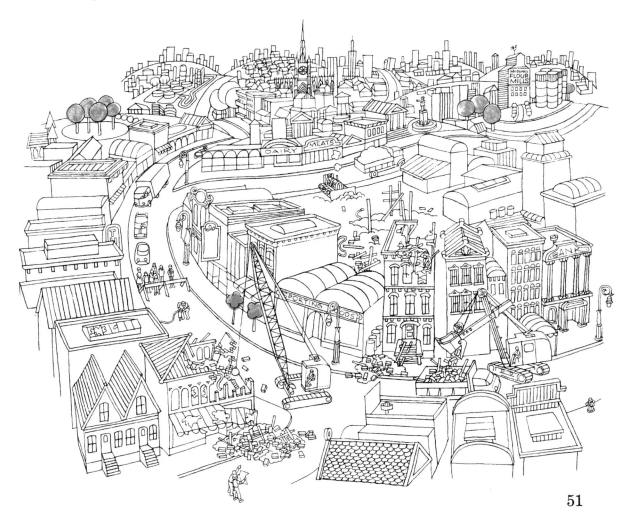

How will people move about in the cities of tomorrow?

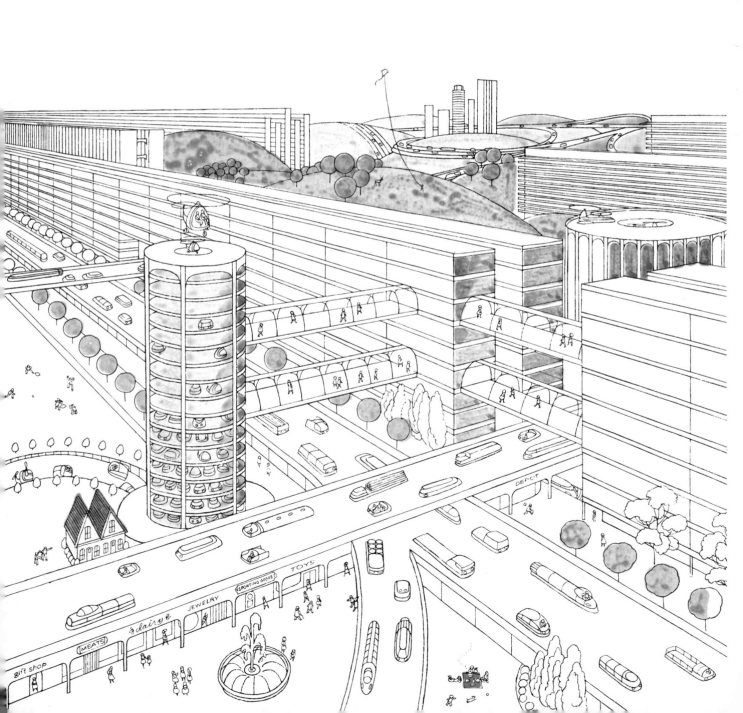

Your family and the community

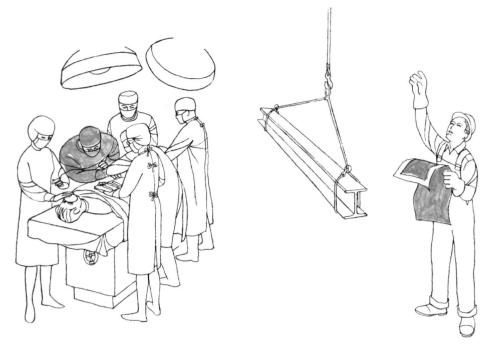

Your family is an important part of the community. Think about the work your father does. How is it important? He may work in your community or in another area, while someone from another town works in yours. The important thing is that all people, working together, provide food, clothing, shelter, gas and electricity, water, and many other services for the use of everyone.

Your mother is a community worker whether she works away from your house or stays at home. Some mothers work in stores. Others work in factories that make radios or instruments for our space age world. Many mothers are teachers.

Have you ever followed your mother through the day's work? She walks miles, drives miles, and does everything from cooking, sewing, and washing, to gardening, repairing, and nursing.

The work your mother and father do to earn money and manage your home is only part of the service they do for your community. They are good citizens who vote in elections, obey laws, and pay taxes.

Perhaps your father belongs to a group that tries to make your town more beautiful, or a group who helps boys.

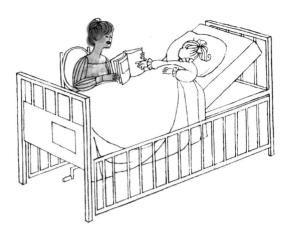

How does your mother help? Perhaps she spends some of her

time reading to children in the hospital or working at the church.

Maybe she belongs to a group that helps your school.

She might work to help elect the person she thinks should be on

the city council.

You, too, are an important person. Your most important job is going to school.

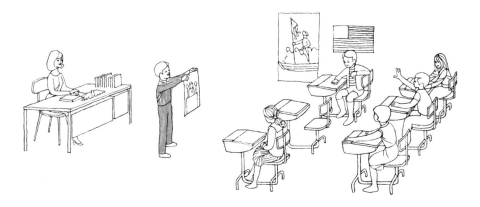

Every day there is more to learn and discover so you can become a good citizen in the community of the future. As you learn about numbers, think about how you might use them when you are grown.

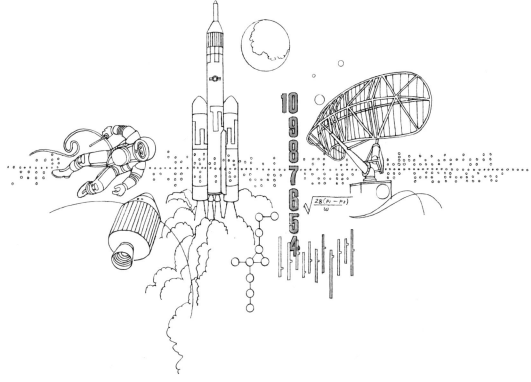

What do you need to know about your country and the world?

In how many ways will it be important to know how to read?

You have other jobs to do to help your community. What can you do in your neighborhood to make it more beautiful? How can you and your friends help other people? What projects can you and your class do to make your community a better place?